G000075039

Tumblr posts planner

This book belongs to:

TUMBLR POSTS *PLANNER*

POST

POST NUMBER _____

POST DATE _____

NOTES _____
_____

POST

POST NUMBER _____

POST DATE _____

NOTES _____
_____

POST

POST NUMBER _____

POST DATE _____

NOTES _____
_____

TUMBLR POSTS *PLANNER*

POST

_____
_____
_____
_____

POST NUMBER _____

POST DATE _____

NOTES _____
_____

POST

_____
_____
_____
_____

POST NUMBER _____

POST DATE _____

NOTES _____
_____

POST

_____
_____
_____
_____

POST NUMBER _____

POST DATE _____

NOTES _____
_____

TUMBLR POSTS *PLANNER*

POST

_____
_____
_____
_____

POST NUMBER _____

POST DATE _____

NOTES _____
_____

POST

_____
_____
_____
_____

POST NUMBER _____

POST DATE _____

NOTES _____
_____

POST

_____
_____
_____
_____

POST NUMBER _____

POST DATE _____

NOTES _____
_____

TUMBLR POSTS *PLANNER*

POST

POST NUMBER _____

POST DATE _____

NOTES _____
_____

POST

POST NUMBER _____

POST DATE _____

NOTES _____
_____

POST

POST NUMBER _____

POST DATE _____

NOTES _____
_____

TUMBLR POSTS *PLANNER*

POST

_____
_____
_____
_____

POST NUMBER _____

POST DATE _____

NOTES _____
_____

POST

_____
_____
_____
_____

POST NUMBER _____

POST DATE _____

NOTES _____
_____

POST

_____
_____
_____
_____

POST NUMBER _____

POST DATE _____

NOTES _____
_____

TUMBLR POSTS *PLANNER*

POST

POST NUMBER _____

POST DATE _____

NOTES _____
_____

POST

POST NUMBER _____

POST DATE _____

NOTES _____
_____

POST

POST NUMBER _____

POST DATE _____

NOTES _____
_____

TUMBLR POSTS *PLANNER*

POST
_____
_____
_____
_____

POST NUMBER _____

POST DATE _____

NOTES _____
_____

POST
_____
_____
_____
_____

POST NUMBER _____

POST DATE _____

NOTES _____
_____

POST
_____
_____
_____
_____

POST NUMBER _____

POST DATE _____

NOTES _____
_____

TUMBLR POSTS *PLANNER*

POST

POST NUMBER _____

POST DATE _____

NOTES _____
_____

POST

POST NUMBER _____

POST DATE _____

NOTES _____
_____

POST

POST NUMBER _____

POST DATE _____

NOTES _____
_____

TUMBLR POSTS *PLANNER*

POST

_____
_____
_____
_____
_____

POST NUMBER _____

POST DATE _____

NOTES _____
_____

POST

_____
_____
_____
_____
_____

POST NUMBER _____

POST DATE _____

NOTES _____
_____

POST

_____
_____
_____
_____
_____

POST NUMBER _____

POST DATE _____

NOTES _____
_____

TUMBLR POSTS *PLANNER*

POST

POST NUMBER _____

POST DATE _____

NOTES _____
_____

POST

POST NUMBER _____

POST DATE _____

NOTES _____
_____

POST

POST NUMBER _____

POST DATE _____

NOTES _____
_____

TUMBLR POSTS *PLANNER*

POST

POST NUMBER _____

POST DATE _____

NOTES _____

POST

POST NUMBER _____

POST DATE _____

NOTES _____

POST

POST NUMBER _____

POST DATE _____

NOTES _____

TUMBLR POSTS *PLANNER*

POST

_____
_____
_____
_____
_____

POST NUMBER _____

POST DATE _____

NOTES _____
_____

POST

_____
_____
_____
_____
_____

POST NUMBER _____

POST DATE _____

NOTES _____
_____

POST

_____
_____
_____
_____
_____

POST NUMBER _____

POST DATE _____

NOTES _____
_____

TUMBLR POSTS *PLANNER*

POST

_____
_____
_____
_____

POST NUMBER _____

POST DATE _____

NOTES _____
_____

POST

_____
_____
_____
_____

POST NUMBER _____

POST DATE _____

NOTES _____
_____

POST

_____
_____
_____
_____

POST NUMBER _____

POST DATE _____

NOTES _____
_____

TUMBLR POSTS *PLANNER*

POST

_____
_____
_____
_____

POST NUMBER _____

POST DATE _____

NOTES _____
_____

POST

_____
_____
_____
_____

POST NUMBER _____

POST DATE _____

NOTES _____
_____

POST

_____
_____
_____
_____

POST NUMBER _____

POST DATE _____

NOTES _____
_____

TUMBLR POSTS *PLANNER*

POST

_____
_____
_____
_____

POST NUMBER _____

POST DATE _____

NOTES _____
_____

POST

_____
_____
_____
_____

POST NUMBER _____

POST DATE _____

NOTES _____
_____

POST

_____
_____
_____
_____

POST NUMBER _____

POST DATE _____

NOTES _____
_____

TUMBLR POSTS *PLANNER*

POST

POST NUMBER _____

POST DATE _____

NOTES _____

POST

POST NUMBER _____

POST DATE _____

NOTES _____

POST

POST NUMBER _____

POST DATE _____

NOTES _____

TUMBLR POSTS *PLANNER*

POST

POST NUMBER _____

POST DATE _____

NOTES _____

_____

POST

POST NUMBER _____

POST DATE _____

NOTES _____

_____

POST

POST NUMBER _____

POST DATE _____

NOTES _____

_____

TUMBLR POSTS *PLANNER*

POST

POST NUMBER _____

POST DATE _____

NOTES _____

POST

POST NUMBER _____

POST DATE _____

NOTES _____

POST

POST NUMBER _____

POST DATE _____

NOTES _____

TUMBLR POSTS *PLANNER*

POST

_____

_____

_____

_____

POST NUMBER _____

POST DATE _____

NOTES _____

_____

POST

_____

_____

_____

_____

POST NUMBER _____

POST DATE _____

NOTES _____

_____

POST

_____

_____

_____

_____

POST NUMBER _____

POST DATE _____

NOTES _____

_____

TUMBLR POSTS *PLANNER*

POST

POST NUMBER _____

POST DATE _____

NOTES _____

POST

POST NUMBER _____

POST DATE _____

NOTES _____

POST

POST NUMBER _____

POST DATE _____

NOTES _____

TUMBLR POSTS *PLANNER*

POST

_____
_____
_____
_____

POST NUMBER _____

POST DATE _____

NOTES _____
_____

POST

_____
_____
_____
_____

POST NUMBER _____

POST DATE _____

NOTES _____
_____

POST

_____
_____
_____
_____

POST NUMBER _____

POST DATE _____

NOTES _____
_____

TUMBLR POSTS *PLANNER*

POST

_____
_____
_____
_____

POST NUMBER _____

POST DATE _____

NOTES _____
_____

POST

_____
_____
_____
_____

POST NUMBER _____

POST DATE _____

NOTES _____
_____

POST

_____
_____
_____
_____

POST NUMBER _____

POST DATE _____

NOTES _____
_____

TUMBLR POSTS *PLANNER*

POST

POST NUMBER _____

POST DATE _____

NOTES _____

_____

POST

POST NUMBER _____

POST DATE _____

NOTES _____

_____

POST

POST NUMBER _____

POST DATE _____

NOTES _____

_____

TUMBLR POSTS *PLANNER*

POST

POST NUMBER _____

POST DATE _____

NOTES _____

POST

POST NUMBER _____

POST DATE _____

NOTES _____

POST

POST NUMBER _____

POST DATE _____

NOTES _____

TUMBLR POSTS *PLANNER*

POST

POST NUMBER _____

POST DATE _____

NOTES _____
_____

POST

POST NUMBER _____

POST DATE _____

NOTES _____
_____

POST

POST NUMBER _____

POST DATE _____

NOTES _____
_____

TUMBLR POSTS *PLANNER*

POST

POST NUMBER _____

POST DATE _____

NOTES _____
_____

POST

POST NUMBER _____

POST DATE _____

NOTES _____
_____

POST

POST NUMBER _____

POST DATE _____

NOTES _____
_____

TUMBLR POSTS *PLANNER*

POST
_____
_____
_____
_____
_____

POST NUMBER _____

POST DATE _____

NOTES _____
_____

POST
_____
_____
_____
_____
_____

POST NUMBER _____

POST DATE _____

NOTES _____
_____

POST
_____
_____
_____
_____
_____

POST NUMBER _____

POST DATE _____

NOTES _____
_____

TUMBLR POSTS *PLANNER*

POST

_____
_____
_____
_____
_____

POST NUMBER _____

POST DATE _____

NOTES _____
_____

POST

_____
_____
_____
_____
_____

POST NUMBER _____

POST DATE _____

NOTES _____
_____

POST

_____
_____
_____
_____
_____

POST NUMBER _____

POST DATE _____

NOTES _____
_____

TUMBLR POSTS *PLANNER*

POST

POST NUMBER _____

POST DATE _____

NOTES _____

POST

POST NUMBER _____

POST DATE _____

NOTES _____

POST

POST NUMBER _____

POST DATE _____

NOTES _____

TUMBLR POSTS *PLANNER*

POST

_____
_____
_____
_____

POST NUMBER _____

POST DATE _____

NOTES _____
_____

POST

_____
_____
_____
_____

POST NUMBER _____

POST DATE _____

NOTES _____
_____

POST

_____
_____
_____
_____

POST NUMBER _____

POST DATE _____

NOTES _____
_____

TUMBLR POSTS *PLANNER*

POST

_____
_____
_____
_____

POST NUMBER _____

POST DATE _____

NOTES _____
_____

POST

_____
_____
_____
_____

POST NUMBER _____

POST DATE _____

NOTES _____
_____

POST

_____
_____
_____
_____

POST NUMBER _____

POST DATE _____

NOTES _____
_____

TUMBLR POSTS *PLANNER*

POST

_____
_____
_____
_____

POST NUMBER _____

POST DATE _____

NOTES _____
_____

POST

_____
_____
_____
_____

POST NUMBER _____

POST DATE _____

NOTES _____
_____

POST

_____
_____
_____
_____

POST NUMBER _____

POST DATE _____

NOTES _____
_____

TUMBLR POSTS *PLANNER*

POST

_____
_____
_____
_____

POST NUMBER _____

POST DATE _____

NOTES _____
_____

POST

_____
_____
_____
_____

POST NUMBER _____

POST DATE _____

NOTES _____
_____

POST

_____
_____
_____
_____

POST NUMBER _____

POST DATE _____

NOTES _____
_____

TUMBLR POSTS *PLANNER*

POST

_____
_____
_____
_____
_____

POST NUMBER _____

POST DATE _____

NOTES _____
_____

POST

_____
_____
_____
_____
_____

POST NUMBER _____

POST DATE _____

NOTES _____
_____

POST

_____
_____
_____
_____
_____

POST NUMBER _____

POST DATE _____

NOTES _____
_____

TUMBLR POSTS *PLANNER*

POST

_____
_____
_____
_____

POST NUMBER _____

POST DATE _____

NOTES _____
_____

POST

_____
_____
_____
_____

POST NUMBER _____

POST DATE _____

NOTES _____
_____

POST

_____
_____
_____
_____

POST NUMBER _____

POST DATE _____

NOTES _____
_____

TUMBLR POSTS *PLANNER*

POST

_____
_____
_____
_____
_____

POST NUMBER _____

POST DATE _____

NOTES _____
_____

POST

_____
_____
_____
_____
_____

POST NUMBER _____

POST DATE _____

NOTES _____
_____

POST

_____
_____
_____
_____
_____

POST NUMBER _____

POST DATE _____

NOTES _____
_____

TUMBLR POSTS *PLANNER*

POST

_____
_____
_____
_____

POST NUMBER _____

POST DATE _____

NOTES _____
_____

POST

_____
_____
_____
_____

POST NUMBER _____

POST DATE _____

NOTES _____
_____

POST

_____
_____
_____
_____

POST NUMBER _____

POST DATE _____

NOTES _____
_____

TUMBLR POSTS *PLANNER*

POST

POST NUMBER _____

POST DATE _____

NOTES _____

POST

POST NUMBER _____

POST DATE _____

NOTES _____

POST

POST NUMBER _____

POST DATE _____

NOTES _____

TUMBLR POSTS *PLANNER*

POST

_____

_____

_____

_____

POST NUMBER _____

POST DATE _____

NOTES _____

_____

POST

_____

_____

_____

_____

POST NUMBER _____

POST DATE _____

NOTES _____

_____

POST

_____

_____

_____

_____

POST NUMBER _____

POST DATE _____

NOTES _____

_____

TUMBLR POSTS *PLANNER*

POST

_____
_____
_____
_____
_____

POST NUMBER _____

POST DATE _____

NOTES _____
_____

POST

_____
_____
_____
_____
_____

POST NUMBER _____

POST DATE _____

NOTES _____
_____

POST

_____
_____
_____
_____
_____

POST NUMBER _____

POST DATE _____

NOTES _____
_____

TUMBLR POSTS *PLANNER*

POST

_____
_____
_____
_____
_____

POST NUMBER _____

POST DATE _____

NOTES _____
_____

POST

_____
_____
_____
_____
_____

POST NUMBER _____

POST DATE _____

NOTES _____
_____

POST

_____
_____
_____
_____
_____

POST NUMBER _____

POST DATE _____

NOTES _____
_____

TUMBLR POSTS *PLANNER*

POST

_____
_____
_____
_____

POST NUMBER _____

POST DATE _____

NOTES _____
_____

POST

_____
_____
_____
_____

POST NUMBER _____

POST DATE _____

NOTES _____
_____

POST

_____
_____
_____
_____

POST NUMBER _____

POST DATE _____

NOTES _____
_____

TUMBLR POSTS *PLANNER*

POST

POST NUMBER _____

POST DATE _____

NOTES _____

_____

POST

POST NUMBER _____

POST DATE _____

NOTES _____

_____

POST

POST NUMBER _____

POST DATE _____

NOTES _____

_____

TUMBLR POSTS *PLANNER*

POST

_____

_____

_____

_____

POST NUMBER _____

POST DATE _____

NOTES _____

_____

POST

_____

_____

_____

_____

POST NUMBER _____

POST DATE _____

NOTES _____

_____

POST

_____

_____

_____

_____

POST NUMBER _____

POST DATE _____

NOTES _____

_____

TUMBLR POSTS *PLANNER*

POST

POST NUMBER _____

POST DATE _____

NOTES _____
_____

POST

POST NUMBER _____

POST DATE _____

NOTES _____
_____

POST

POST NUMBER _____

POST DATE _____

NOTES _____
_____

TUMBLR POSTS *PLANNER*

POST

_____
_____
_____
_____

POST NUMBER _____

POST DATE _____

NOTES _____
_____

POST

_____
_____
_____
_____

POST NUMBER _____

POST DATE _____

NOTES _____
_____

POST

_____
_____
_____
_____

POST NUMBER _____

POST DATE _____

NOTES _____
_____

TUMBLR POSTS *PLANNER*

POST

_____
_____
_____
_____

POST NUMBER _____

POST DATE _____

NOTES _____
_____

POST

_____
_____
_____
_____

POST NUMBER _____

POST DATE _____

NOTES _____
_____

POST

_____
_____
_____
_____

POST NUMBER _____

POST DATE _____

NOTES _____
_____

TUMBLR POSTS *PLANNER*

POST

_____
_____
_____
_____

POST NUMBER _____

POST DATE _____

NOTES _____
_____

POST

_____
_____
_____
_____

POST NUMBER _____

POST DATE _____

NOTES _____
_____

POST

_____
_____
_____
_____

POST NUMBER _____

POST DATE _____

NOTES _____
_____

TUMBLR POSTS *PLANNER*

POST

_____

_____

_____

_____

POST NUMBER _____

POST DATE _____

NOTES _____
_____

POST

_____

_____

_____

_____

POST NUMBER _____

POST DATE _____

NOTES _____
_____

POST

_____

_____

_____

_____

POST NUMBER _____

POST DATE _____

NOTES _____
_____

TUMBLR POSTS *PLANNER*

POST

_____
_____
_____
_____

POST NUMBER _____

POST DATE _____

NOTES _____
_____

POST

_____
_____
_____
_____

POST NUMBER _____

POST DATE _____

NOTES _____
_____

POST

_____
_____
_____
_____

POST NUMBER _____

POST DATE _____

NOTES _____
_____

TUMBLR POSTS *PLANNER*

POST

_____
_____
_____
_____

POST NUMBER _____

POST DATE _____

NOTES _____
_____

POST

_____
_____
_____
_____

POST NUMBER _____

POST DATE _____

NOTES _____
_____

POST

_____
_____
_____
_____

POST NUMBER _____

POST DATE _____

NOTES _____
_____

TUMBLR POSTS *PLANNER*

POST

_____
_____
_____
_____
_____

POST NUMBER _____

POST DATE _____

NOTES _____
_____

POST

_____
_____
_____
_____

POST NUMBER _____

POST DATE _____

NOTES _____
_____

POST

_____
_____
_____
_____

POST NUMBER _____

POST DATE _____

NOTES _____
_____

TUMBLR POSTS *PLANNER*

POST

POST NUMBER _____

POST DATE _____

NOTES _____

POST

POST NUMBER _____

POST DATE _____

NOTES _____

POST

POST NUMBER _____

POST DATE _____

NOTES _____

TUMBLR POSTS *PLANNER*

POST

_____

POST NUMBER _____

POST DATE _____

NOTES _____

POST

_____

POST NUMBER _____

POST DATE _____

NOTES _____

POST

_____

POST NUMBER _____

POST DATE _____

NOTES _____

TUMBLR POSTS *PLANNER*

POST

POST NUMBER _____

POST DATE _____

NOTES _____
_____

POST

POST NUMBER _____

POST DATE _____

NOTES _____
_____

POST

POST NUMBER _____

POST DATE _____

NOTES _____
_____

TUMBLR POSTS *PLANNER*

POST

_____
_____
_____
_____

POST NUMBER _____

POST DATE _____

NOTES _____
_____

POST

_____
_____
_____
_____

POST NUMBER _____

POST DATE _____

NOTES _____
_____

POST

_____
_____
_____
_____

POST NUMBER _____

POST DATE _____

NOTES _____
_____

TUMBLR POSTS *PLANNER*

(POST)

_____
_____
_____
_____

POST NUMBER _____

POST DATE _____

NOTES _____
_____

(POST)

_____
_____
_____
_____

POST NUMBER _____

POST DATE _____

NOTES _____
_____

(POST)

_____
_____
_____
_____

POST NUMBER _____

POST DATE _____

NOTES _____
_____

TUMBLR POSTS *PLANNER*

POST

_____
_____
_____
_____

POST NUMBER _____

POST DATE _____

NOTES _____
_____

POST

_____
_____
_____
_____

POST NUMBER _____

POST DATE _____

NOTES _____
_____

POST

_____
_____
_____
_____

POST NUMBER _____

POST DATE _____

NOTES _____
_____

TUMBLR POSTS *PLANNER*

POST

_____
_____
_____
_____

POST NUMBER _____

POST DATE _____

NOTES _____
_____

POST

_____
_____
_____
_____

POST NUMBER _____

POST DATE _____

NOTES _____
_____

POST

_____
_____
_____
_____

POST NUMBER _____

POST DATE _____

NOTES _____
_____

TUMBLR POSTS *PLANNER*

POST

_____
_____
_____
_____

POST NUMBER _____

POST DATE _____

NOTES _____
_____

POST

_____
_____
_____
_____

POST NUMBER _____

POST DATE _____

NOTES _____
_____

POST

_____
_____
_____
_____

POST NUMBER _____

POST DATE _____

NOTES _____
_____

TUMBLR POSTS *PLANNER*

POST

POST NUMBER _____

POST DATE _____

NOTES _____
_____

POST

POST NUMBER _____

POST DATE _____

NOTES _____
_____

POST

POST NUMBER _____

POST DATE _____

NOTES _____
_____

TUMBLR POSTS *PLANNER*

POST

_____
_____
_____
_____
_____

POST NUMBER _____

POST DATE _____

NOTES _____
_____

POST

_____
_____
_____
_____
_____

POST NUMBER _____

POST DATE _____

NOTES _____
_____

POST

_____
_____
_____
_____
_____

POST NUMBER _____

POST DATE _____

NOTES _____
_____

TUMBLR POSTS *PLANNER*

POST

_____
_____
_____
_____

POST NUMBER _____

POST DATE _____

NOTES _____
_____

POST

_____
_____
_____
_____

POST NUMBER _____

POST DATE _____

NOTES _____
_____

POST

_____
_____
_____
_____

POST NUMBER _____

POST DATE _____

NOTES _____
_____

TUMBLR POSTS *PLANNER*

POST

POST NUMBER _____

POST DATE _____

NOTES _____
_____

POST

POST NUMBER _____

POST DATE _____

NOTES _____
_____

POST

POST NUMBER _____

POST DATE _____

NOTES _____
_____

TUMBLR POSTS *PLANNER*

(POST)

POST NUMBER _____

POST DATE _____

NOTES _____

(POST)

POST NUMBER _____

POST DATE _____

NOTES _____

(POST)

POST NUMBER _____

POST DATE _____

NOTES _____

TUMBLR POSTS *PLANNER*

POST

_____

_____

_____

_____

POST NUMBER _____

POST DATE _____

NOTES _____

_____

POST

_____

_____

_____

_____

POST NUMBER _____

POST DATE _____

NOTES _____

_____

POST

_____

_____

_____

_____

POST NUMBER _____

POST DATE _____

NOTES _____

_____

TUMBLR POSTS *PLANNER*

POST

_____

_____

_____

_____

POST NUMBER _____

POST DATE _____

NOTES _____
_____

POST

_____

_____

_____

_____

POST NUMBER _____

POST DATE _____

NOTES _____
_____

POST

_____

_____

_____

_____

POST NUMBER _____

POST DATE _____

NOTES _____
_____

TUMBLR POSTS *PLANNER*

POST

_____
_____
_____
_____

POST NUMBER _____

POST DATE _____

NOTES _____
_____

POST

_____
_____
_____
_____

POST NUMBER _____

POST DATE _____

NOTES _____
_____

POST

_____
_____
_____
_____

POST NUMBER _____

POST DATE _____

NOTES _____
_____

TUMBLR POSTS *PLANNER*

POST

POST NUMBER _____

POST DATE _____

NOTES _____
_____

POST

POST NUMBER _____

POST DATE _____

NOTES _____
_____

POST

POST NUMBER _____

POST DATE _____

NOTES _____
_____

TUMBLR POSTS *PLANNER*

POST

_____
_____
_____
_____

POST NUMBER _____

POST DATE _____

NOTES _____
_____

POST

_____
_____
_____
_____

POST NUMBER _____

POST DATE _____

NOTES _____
_____

POST

_____
_____
_____
_____

POST NUMBER _____

POST DATE _____

NOTES _____
_____

TUMBLR POSTS *PLANNER*

(POST)

_____
_____
_____
_____

POST NUMBER _____

POST DATE _____

NOTES _____
_____

(POST)

_____
_____
_____
_____

POST NUMBER _____

POST DATE _____

NOTES _____
_____

(POST)

_____
_____
_____
_____

POST NUMBER _____

POST DATE _____

NOTES _____
_____

TUMBLR POSTS *PLANNER*

POST

_____
_____
_____

POST NUMBER _____

POST DATE _____

NOTES _____
_____

POST

_____
_____
_____
_____

POST NUMBER _____

POST DATE _____

NOTES _____
_____

POST

_____
_____
_____

POST NUMBER _____

POST DATE _____

NOTES _____
_____

TUMBLR POSTS *PLANNER*

POST
_____
_____
_____
_____
_____

POST NUMBER _____

POST DATE _____

NOTES _____
_____

POST
_____
_____
_____
_____
_____

POST NUMBER _____

POST DATE _____

NOTES _____
_____

POST
_____
_____
_____
_____
_____

POST NUMBER _____

POST DATE _____

NOTES _____
_____

TUMBLR POSTS *PLANNER*

POST

_____
_____
_____
_____

POST NUMBER _____

POST DATE _____

NOTES _____
_____

POST

_____
_____
_____
_____

POST NUMBER _____

POST DATE _____

NOTES _____
_____

POST

_____
_____
_____
_____

POST NUMBER _____

POST DATE _____

NOTES _____
_____

TUMBLR POSTS *PLANNER*

POST

POST NUMBER _____

POST DATE _____

NOTES _____
_____

POST

POST NUMBER _____

POST DATE _____

NOTES _____
_____

POST

POST NUMBER _____

POST DATE _____

NOTES _____
_____

TUMBLR POSTS *PLANNER*

POST

_____
_____
_____
_____

POST NUMBER _____

POST DATE _____

NOTES _____
_____

POST

_____
_____
_____
_____

POST NUMBER _____

POST DATE _____

NOTES _____
_____

POST

_____
_____
_____
_____

POST NUMBER _____

POST DATE _____

NOTES _____
_____

TUMBLR POSTS *PLANNER*

POST

_____

_____

_____

_____

POST NUMBER _____

POST DATE _____

NOTES _____
_____

POST

_____

_____

_____

_____

POST NUMBER _____

POST DATE _____

NOTES _____
_____

POST

_____

_____

_____

_____

POST NUMBER _____

POST DATE _____

NOTES _____
_____

TUMBLR POSTS *PLANNER*

POST

_____
_____
_____
_____

POST NUMBER _____

POST DATE _____

NOTES _____
_____

POST

_____
_____
_____
_____

POST NUMBER _____

POST DATE _____

NOTES _____
_____

POST

_____
_____
_____
_____

POST NUMBER _____

POST DATE _____

NOTES _____
_____

TUMBLR POSTS *PLANNER*

POST

_____
_____
_____
_____

POST NUMBER _____

POST DATE _____

NOTES _____
_____

POST

_____
_____
_____
_____

POST NUMBER _____

POST DATE _____

NOTES _____
_____

POST

_____
_____
_____
_____

POST NUMBER _____

POST DATE _____

NOTES _____
_____

TUMBLR POSTS *PLANNER*

POST

_____

_____

_____

_____

POST NUMBER _____

POST DATE _____

NOTES _____

_____

POST

_____

_____

_____

_____

POST NUMBER _____

POST DATE _____

NOTES _____

_____

POST

_____

_____

_____

_____

POST NUMBER _____

POST DATE _____

NOTES _____

_____

TUMBLR POSTS *PLANNER*

POST

_____
_____
_____
_____

POST NUMBER _____

POST DATE _____

NOTES _____
_____

POST

_____
_____
_____
_____

POST NUMBER _____

POST DATE _____

NOTES _____
_____

POST

_____
_____
_____
_____

POST NUMBER _____

POST DATE _____

NOTES _____
_____

TUMBLR POSTS *PLANNER*

POST

POST NUMBER _____

POST DATE _____

NOTES _____
_____

POST

POST NUMBER _____

POST DATE _____

NOTES _____
_____

POST

POST NUMBER _____

POST DATE _____

NOTES _____
_____

TUMBLR POSTS *PLANNER*

POST

POST NUMBER _____

POST DATE _____

NOTES _____
_____

POST

POST NUMBER _____

POST DATE _____

NOTES _____
_____

POST

POST NUMBER _____

POST DATE _____

NOTES _____
_____

TUMBLR POSTS *PLANNER*

POST

_____
_____
_____
_____

POST NUMBER _____

POST DATE _____

NOTES _____
_____

POST

_____
_____
_____
_____

POST NUMBER _____

POST DATE _____

NOTES _____
_____

POST

_____
_____
_____
_____

POST NUMBER _____

POST DATE _____

NOTES _____
_____

TUMBLR POSTS *PLANNER*

POST

_____
_____
_____
_____

POST NUMBER _____

POST DATE _____

NOTES _____
_____

POST

_____
_____
_____
_____

POST NUMBER _____

POST DATE _____

NOTES _____
_____

POST

_____
_____
_____
_____

POST NUMBER _____

POST DATE _____

NOTES _____
_____

TUMBLR POSTS *PLANNER*

POST

_____
_____
_____
_____

POST NUMBER _____

POST DATE _____

NOTES _____
_____

POST

_____
_____
_____
_____

POST NUMBER _____

POST DATE _____

NOTES _____
_____

POST

_____
_____
_____
_____

POST NUMBER _____

POST DATE _____

NOTES _____
_____

TUMBLR POSTS *PLANNER*

POST

_____
_____
_____
_____

POST NUMBER _____

POST DATE _____

NOTES _____
_____

POST

_____
_____
_____
_____

POST NUMBER _____

POST DATE _____

NOTES _____
_____

POST

_____
_____
_____
_____

POST NUMBER _____

POST DATE _____

NOTES _____
_____

TUMBLR POSTS *PLANNER*

POST

POST NUMBER _____

POST DATE _____

NOTES _____
_____

POST

POST NUMBER _____

POST DATE _____

NOTES _____
_____

POST

POST NUMBER _____

POST DATE _____

NOTES _____
_____

TUMBLR POSTS *PLANNER*

POST
_____
_____
_____
_____
_____
_____

POST NUMBER _____

POST DATE _____

NOTES _____
_____

POST
_____
_____
_____
_____
_____
_____

POST NUMBER _____

POST DATE _____

NOTES _____
_____

POST
_____
_____
_____
_____
_____
_____

POST NUMBER _____

POST DATE _____

NOTES _____
_____

TUMBLR POSTS *PLANNER*

POST

_____
_____
_____
_____

POST NUMBER _____

POST DATE _____

NOTES _____
_____

POST

_____
_____
_____
_____

POST NUMBER _____

POST DATE _____

NOTES _____
_____

POST

_____
_____
_____
_____

POST NUMBER _____

POST DATE _____

NOTES _____
_____

TUMBLR POSTS *PLANNER*

POST

_____
_____
_____
_____

POST NUMBER _____

POST DATE _____

NOTES _____
_____

POST

_____
_____
_____
_____

POST NUMBER _____

POST DATE _____

NOTES _____
_____

POST

_____
_____
_____
_____

POST NUMBER _____

POST DATE _____

NOTES _____
_____

TUMBLR POSTS *PLANNER*

POST

_____
_____
_____
_____

POST NUMBER _____

POST DATE _____

NOTES _____
_____

POST

_____
_____
_____
_____

POST NUMBER _____

POST DATE _____

NOTES _____
_____

POST

_____
_____
_____
_____

POST NUMBER _____

POST DATE _____

NOTES _____
_____

TUMBLR POSTS *PLANNER*

POST

POST NUMBER _____

POST DATE _____

NOTES _____

_____

POST

POST NUMBER _____

POST DATE _____

NOTES _____

_____

POST

POST NUMBER _____

POST DATE _____

NOTES _____

_____

TUMBLR POSTS *PLANNER*

POST

POST NUMBER _____

POST DATE _____

NOTES _____

POST

POST NUMBER _____

POST DATE _____

NOTES _____

POST

POST NUMBER _____

POST DATE _____

NOTES _____

TUMBLR POSTS *PLANNER*

POST

POST NUMBER _____

POST DATE _____

NOTES _____

_____

POST

POST NUMBER _____

POST DATE _____

NOTES _____

_____

POST

POST NUMBER _____

POST DATE _____

NOTES _____

_____

TUMBLR POSTS *PLANNER*

POST

_____

_____

_____

_____

POST NUMBER _____

POST DATE _____

NOTES _____
_____

POST

_____

_____

_____

_____

POST NUMBER _____

POST DATE _____

NOTES _____
_____

POST

_____

_____

_____

_____

POST NUMBER _____

POST DATE _____

NOTES _____
_____

TUMBLR POSTS *PLANNER*

POST

_____
_____
_____
_____

POST NUMBER _____

POST DATE _____

NOTES _____
_____

POST

_____
_____
_____
_____

POST NUMBER _____

POST DATE _____

NOTES _____
_____

POST

_____
_____
_____
_____

POST NUMBER _____

POST DATE _____

NOTES _____
_____

TUMBLR POSTS *PLANNER*

POST

_____
_____
_____
_____

POST NUMBER _____

POST DATE _____

NOTES _____
_____

POST

_____
_____
_____
_____

POST NUMBER _____

POST DATE _____

NOTES _____
_____

POST

_____
_____
_____
_____

POST NUMBER _____

POST DATE _____

NOTES _____
_____

TUMBLR POSTS *PLANNER*

POST

POST NUMBER _____

POST DATE _____

NOTES _____
_____

POST

POST NUMBER _____

POST DATE _____

NOTES _____
_____

POST

POST NUMBER _____

POST DATE _____

NOTES _____
_____

TUMBLR POSTS *PLANNER*

POST

POST NUMBER _____

POST DATE _____

NOTES _____

POST

POST NUMBER _____

POST DATE _____

NOTES _____

POST

POST NUMBER _____

POST DATE _____

NOTES _____

TUMBLR POSTS *PLANNER*

POST

_____
_____
_____
_____

POST NUMBER _____

POST DATE _____

NOTES _____
_____

POST

_____
_____
_____
_____

POST NUMBER _____

POST DATE _____

NOTES _____
_____

POST

_____
_____
_____
_____

POST NUMBER _____

POST DATE _____

NOTES _____
_____

TUMBLR POSTS *PLANNER*

POST

POST NUMBER _____

POST DATE _____

NOTES _____

POST

POST NUMBER _____

POST DATE _____

NOTES _____

POST

POST NUMBER _____

POST DATE _____

NOTES _____

TUMBLR POSTS *PLANNER*

POST

_____
_____
_____
_____

POST NUMBER _____

POST DATE _____

NOTES _____
_____

POST

_____
_____
_____
_____

POST NUMBER _____

POST DATE _____

NOTES _____
_____

POST

_____
_____
_____
_____

POST NUMBER _____

POST DATE _____

NOTES _____
_____

TUMBLR POSTS *PLANNER*

POST

_____

_____

_____

_____

POST NUMBER _____

POST DATE _____

NOTES _____

_____

POST

_____

_____

_____

_____

POST NUMBER _____

POST DATE _____

NOTES _____

_____

POST

_____

_____

_____

_____

POST NUMBER _____

POST DATE _____

NOTES _____

_____

TUMBLR POSTS *PLANNER*

POST

_____
_____
_____
_____
_____

POST NUMBER _____

POST DATE _____

NOTES _____
_____

POST

_____
_____
_____
_____
_____

POST NUMBER _____

POST DATE _____

NOTES _____
_____

POST

_____
_____
_____
_____
_____

POST NUMBER _____

POST DATE _____

NOTES _____
_____

TUMBLR POSTS *PLANNER*

POST

_____
_____
_____
_____

POST NUMBER _____

POST DATE _____

NOTES _____
_____

POST

_____
_____
_____
_____

POST NUMBER _____

POST DATE _____

NOTES _____
_____

POST

_____
_____
_____
_____

POST NUMBER _____

POST DATE _____

NOTES _____
_____

TUMBLR POSTS *PLANNER*

POST

POST NUMBER _____

POST DATE _____

NOTES _____
_____

POST

POST NUMBER _____

POST DATE _____

NOTES _____
_____

POST

POST NUMBER _____

POST DATE _____

NOTES _____
_____

TUMBLR POSTS *PLANNER*

POST

_____
_____
_____
_____
_____

POST NUMBER _____

POST DATE _____

NOTES _____
_____

POST

_____
_____
_____
_____
_____

POST NUMBER _____

POST DATE _____

NOTES _____
_____

POST

_____
_____
_____
_____
_____

POST NUMBER _____

POST DATE _____

NOTES _____
_____

TUMBLR POSTS *PLANNER*

POST

_____
_____
_____
_____
_____

POST NUMBER _____

POST DATE _____

NOTES _____
_____

POST

_____
_____
_____
_____
_____

POST NUMBER _____

POST DATE _____

NOTES _____
_____

POST

_____
_____
_____
_____
_____

POST NUMBER _____

POST DATE _____

NOTES _____
_____

TUMBLR POSTS *PLANNER*

POST

_____
_____
_____
_____
_____

POST NUMBER _____

POST DATE _____

NOTES _____
_____

POST

_____
_____
_____
_____
_____

POST NUMBER _____

POST DATE _____

NOTES _____
_____

POST

_____
_____
_____
_____
_____

POST NUMBER _____

POST DATE _____

NOTES _____
_____

TUMBLR POSTS *PLANNER*

POST

POST NUMBER _____

POST DATE _____

NOTES _____
_____

POST

POST NUMBER _____

POST DATE _____

NOTES _____
_____

POST

POST NUMBER _____

POST DATE _____

NOTES _____
_____

TUMBLR POSTS *PLANNER*

POST

POST NUMBER _____

POST DATE _____

NOTES _____
_____

POST

POST NUMBER _____

POST DATE _____

NOTES _____
_____

POST

POST NUMBER _____

POST DATE _____

NOTES _____
_____

TUMBLR POSTS *PLANNER*

POST

POST NUMBER _____

POST DATE _____

NOTES _____
_____

POST

POST NUMBER _____

POST DATE _____

NOTES _____
_____

POST

POST NUMBER _____

POST DATE _____

NOTES _____
_____

TUMBLR POSTS *PLANNER*

POST

POST NUMBER _____

POST DATE _____

NOTES _____

POST

POST NUMBER _____

POST DATE _____

NOTES _____

POST

POST NUMBER _____

POST DATE _____

NOTES _____

TUMBLR POSTS *PLANNER*

POST

_____
_____
_____
_____

POST NUMBER _____

POST DATE _____

NOTES _____
_____

POST

_____
_____
_____
_____

POST NUMBER _____

POST DATE _____

NOTES _____
_____

POST

_____
_____
_____
_____

POST NUMBER _____

POST DATE _____

NOTES _____
_____

TUMBLR POSTS *PLANNER*

POST

_____
_____
_____
_____

POST NUMBER _____

POST DATE _____

NOTES _____
_____

POST

_____
_____
_____
_____

POST NUMBER _____

POST DATE _____

NOTES _____
_____

POST

_____
_____
_____
_____

POST NUMBER _____

POST DATE _____

NOTES _____
_____

TUMBLR POSTS *PLANNER*

POST

_____
_____
_____
_____

POST NUMBER _____

POST DATE _____

NOTES _____
_____

POST

_____
_____
_____
_____

POST NUMBER _____

POST DATE _____

NOTES _____
_____

POST

_____
_____
_____
_____

POST NUMBER _____

POST DATE _____

NOTES _____
_____

TUMBLR POSTS *PLANNER*

POST

_____
_____
_____
_____
_____

POST NUMBER _____

POST DATE _____

NOTES _____
_____

POST

_____
_____
_____
_____
_____

POST NUMBER _____

POST DATE _____

NOTES _____
_____

POST

_____
_____
_____
_____
_____

POST NUMBER _____

POST DATE _____

NOTES _____
_____

TUMBLR POSTS *PLANNER*

POST

POST NUMBER _____

POST DATE _____

NOTES _____

POST

POST NUMBER _____

POST DATE _____

NOTES _____

POST

POST NUMBER _____

POST DATE _____

NOTES _____